QUAKE

by Anthony Booth

SAMUEL FRENCH

FOR PRODUCTION ENQUIRIES

UNITED KINGDOM AND WORLD
EXCLUDING NORTH AMERICA
licensing@concordtheatricals.co.uk

020-7054-7298

NORTH AMERICA
info@concordtheatricals.com
1-866-979-0447

Each title is subject to availability from Concord Theatricals, depending upon country of performance.

written permission of the publisher. No one shall share this title, or part of this title, to any social media or file hosting websites.

The moral right of Anthony Booth to be identified as author of this work has been asserted in accordance with Section 77 of the Copyright, Designs and Patents Act 1988.

USE OF COPYRIGHTED MUSIC

A licence issued by Concord Theatricals to perform this play does not include permission to use the incidental music specified in this publication. In the United Kingdom: Where the place of performance is already licensed by the PERFORMING RIGHT SOCIETY (PRS) a return of the music used must be made to them. If the place of performance is not so licensed then application should be made to PRS for Music (www.prsformusic.com). A separate and additional licence from PHONOGRAPHIC PERFORMANCE LTD (www.ppluk.com) may be needed whenever commercial recordings are used. Outside the United Kingdom: Please contact the appropriate music licensing authority in your territory for the rights to any incidental music.

USE OF COPYRIGHTED THIRD-PARTY MATERIALS

Licensees are solely responsible for obtaining formal written permission from copyright owners to use copyrighted third-party materials (e.g., artworks, logos) in the performance of this play and are strongly cautioned to do so. If no such permission is obtained by the licensee, then the licensee must use only original materials that the licensee owns and controls. Licensees are solely responsible and liable for clearances of all third-party copyrighted materials, and shall indemnify the copyright owners of the play(s) and their licensing agent, Concord Theatricals Ltd., against any costs, expenses, losses and liabilities arising from the use of such copyrighted third-party materials by licensees.

IMPORTANT BILLING AND CREDIT REQUIREMENTS

If you have obtained performance rights to this title, please refer to your licensing agreement for important billing and credit requirements.

CHARACTERS

Marcia

Pearl

Sue

Sheena

Ellen

The action takes place in a bare room at an agricultural station set in the heart of the Pampas in the Province of Marimba, South America

Scene 1   Evening of the first day
Scene 2   Dawn, the following morning
Scene 3   Two hours later
Scene 4   Evening of the same day
Scene 5   Dawn, four days later

Time—the present

Production notes

This play, an established festival winner, deals with a group of women under stress. The characters are clearly defined and should be studied in detail in order to get the best reaction to each setback as the play progresses. One should be able to see almost from the start the animosity between Marcia and Ellen which accounts for a lot of the tension in the story and this should be played hard. There are many telling pauses which should not be hurried. On the other hand, there are moments of almost hysteria, such as when the tremor occurs in the beginning, the apparent arrival of the rescue plane and the breaking of the dam at the end, which should be played wildly without restraint.

Everything the women use is for the most part grubby. In the original production plastic buckets were used for carrying the water and old pottery mugs for drinking etc. For dressing, odd items such as a tattered sombrero, a stock whip, an old simple bridle and a canvas water sling were hung at odd places on the walls of the room. The table top, beer crates and chairs were heavily dusted with talcum powder so that when they fell in the tremor in the opening scene there was a cloud of "dust". The tremor should be carefully rehearsed as this is most effective and quite frightening to watch. The women should take one step forward, two back and then three forward, all with a swaying movement, finally collapsing and taking the table and chairs, etc., down with them.

As from the start of Scene 2, the women unconsciously stake out their territory in the room which they retain until the end of the play. Sue has her box downstage right. Marcia takes the chair situated upstage right centre. Sheena takes over the chair at the left end of the table and puts her carrier, etc., by her feet. Ellen puts her box downstage left. Pearl has no territory as such but always gravitates to above the table.

All the women wore light cotton dresses and it helps if there is evidence of damage in some sort in the form of tears which occurred when they scrambled from the damaged vehicle. When they first appear they are also covered in dust and dirt which can be easily wiped clean for the ensuing scenes. All the women are sun-tanned and none wears stockings or tights with the exception of Ellen, who as "boss" feels she should keep up some form of standard. She wears tights but they are holed or laddered because of the situation.

The theme music for the play was "The Light of Experience" by Gheorghe Zamfir.

QUAKE

Scene 1

A bare room at an agricultural station set in the heart of the Pampas in the Province of Marimba, South America. Evening

The place is used for an overnight stoppage point by the vaqueros when they bring the herds down to the station for inoculation. It is very rough, very dirty and obviously never cleaned. Odd bits of rubbish lie around on the floor, and cut-out pictures, roughly torn from "girlie" magazines, adorn the walls. An opening leads to the cattle yards, with a wide open window below it, and another to the bunkroom. Furniture consists of an old dirty rough wooden table, three old kitchen tables lying on the floor, and a pile of beer crates. (See plan of set on p. 39)

When the Curtain *rises the room is empty. After a few moments agitated voices are heard in the distance, growing louder as the women approach the building. Sue, an attractive woman of about thirty, enters quickly, looks round, and calls*

Sue (*urgently*) Anyone here? (*Seeing the room empty, she runs across and into the bunkroom*) Is there anyone here?

There is no answer

>*After a moment Marcia and Sheena enter, supporting Pearl, who walks unsteadily as if in a daze. Ellen follows, but hesitates, standing just inside the opening. Marcia, Pearl and Sheena could be any age between thirty and forty-five; Ellen appears to be slightly older. As they enter, Sue reappears from the bunkroom*

Marcia (*curtly*) Chair, Sue.

Sue moves quickly to a chair which is lying on the floor. She stands it up. They put Pearl carefully in the chair

Ellen (*curtly*) Put her head between her knees.
Marcia (*shortly*) Why?
Ellen (*curtly*) Don't argue. Do it.

Marcia stares at Ellen belligerently for a moment then helps Pearl

Marcia (*gently*) Put your head down between your knees, we'll help you.
Pearl (*very dazedly*) Do what?
Marcia (*gently*) Lower your head.

Marcia gently pushes Pearl's head down. There is a pause then Pearl half raises her head

Pearl Oh God, I'm going to throw up.

Sheena turns away very distastefully

Sheena Oh I hope not.
Marcia (*angrily*) If it upsets you get out of the bloody way.

Sheena moves a pace away, turning her back on them

(*Quietly*) Fire ahead if it makes you feel any better.

Sue (*quietly*) I'll see if I can find something.

She looks about her but there does not appear to be anything suitable. Pearl retches a little, then speaks

Pearl Don't bother, I'm O.K. now. (*She sits up and feels the top of her head*) Cor, my ruddy head. (*She examines her hand for blood*)
Marcia You haven't cut yourself, there is no blood.

Pearl glances round, blinking. She seems to have a little difficulty in focussing

Pearl What is this place?
Sue We don't know, we just saw this building and made for it.
Ellen It's an agricultural station of sorts.
Sheena How do you know that?
Ellen I saw a notice outside as we came in. I'll go and check.

Ellen goes out to the yards

Pearl What the hell are we doing in an agricultural station?
Sue Because of the accident.
Pearl (*dully*) What accident?

They all look at one another

Sue (*quietly*) She's concussed.
Marcia (*gently*) Pearl, what *do* you remember?

Pearl thinks for a moment, then shakes her head

Pearl (*dully*) Nothing.
Sheena Do you know who we are?
Pearl Don't be daft, of course I do.
Sheena Well, that's something.

Marcia half kneels beside Pearl

Marcia I'll go back to the beginning, but stop me if you remember
   anything.
Pearl Right.
Marcia The men left early this morning to go down to the coast
   for a couple of days to do a rough survey on the new dam.
Pearl Dam?
Sue Yes, the one they are proposing . . .
Marcia Never mind, its unimportant. (*To Pearl*) We all decided
   to go to Marimba for the day to do some shopping.

She waits, but Pearl shakes her head

   Manuel drove us all there in the station wagon.
Pearl This place—Mar . . . Mar . . .
Sheena Marimba?
Pearl Yes. How far is it?
Sue About eighty miles.
Marcia We had an early lunch then went shopping. Do you
   remember any of that?
Pearl No.
Marcia We left about four o'clock to come back and about
   half way, it happened.
Pearl (*puzzled*) What happened?
Sue The earthquake. *Surely* you must remember *that*.

Pearl looks at them unbelievingly. Sheena kneels beside her

Sheena You *must* remember. The road suddenly disappeared in
   front of us and the whole hillside came crashing down into the
   river.
Pearl Good lord!

Marcia Manuel pulled off the road on to a track which led towards the mountains. We had gone about a mile and were just going through a rock cutting when the second shake came which brought down some huge boulders onto the bonnet and cab of the vehicle. We were all sitting in the back but you were up front with Manuel, and that's where you got hit on the head when the roof caved in.

She waits, but Pearl cannot recall anything

Sue We managed to pull you clear then saw this place in the distance and made for it.

Pearl concentrates for a moment then speaks quietly

Pearl Where's Manuel?

No-one answers

Well, come on. Where is he?
Marcia He's dead.
Pearl (*frowning*) Oh no.
Marcia A huge rock landed on his side of the cab, he never stood a chance.

Sheena cries quietly. Marcia turns on her vehemently

Oh, for God's sake, Sheena, shut up.
Sheena (*turning on her*) Doesn't it mean anything to you that the man is dead?
Marcia (*harshly*) Of course it does, but he'll be just as dead in ten years' time.
Sheena Haven't you any feelings?
Marcia Of course I have but I can't weep over someone I didn't even know. Right now the important thing is that we are alive and it is up to us to survive somehow.
Sheena (*bitterly*) You are a hard bitch aren't you, Marcia.

Marcia is about to reply when Sue breaks in

Sue O.K., O.K. let's cool it, there's no mileage in this.

The tension subsides and Sheena moves a little towards the table. After a moment Pearl looks round

Pearl Is the old ratbag with us?

Sue (*smiling*) You are feeling better, aren't you?
Pearl Yes.
Sue She went out a moment ago, and for heaven's sake don't
  let her hear you call her that.

Pearl stands

  Take it easy now.

Pearl moves to the table, picks up the chair behind it and sits

Pearl I'm all right now—really. (*She shuts her eyes for a moment*)
  I'm beginning to remember things . . . I bought a frying-pan,
  didn't I?
Sheena Yes.
Pearl That's right, one with a copper bottom to make Bill
  pancakes. Well, that's something, I've remembered my old
  man's name.
Marcia Big deal. Don't try too hard, it will all come back in
  time, the main thing is to . . .

Ellen enters

Ellen I've had a look round . . . (*Seeing Pearl*) Oh, you are better,
  Pearl. I'm so glad.
Sue What did you find?
Ellen Well I was just saying, I've had a look round outside. My
  Spanish is a bit rusty, but as far as I can make out this is a
  government agricultural station.
Sheena For what?
Ellen According to the notices something to do with foot and
  mouth disease. I think they bring the herds down here for in-
  oculation. There is a large area of stockyards on the other side.
Sue That explains it, then. Any sign of anyone?
Ellen No. I've called several times, but there is no answer.
Sue Are there any cattle there now?
Ellen No, but half the stockyard is down.
Sheena So, what do we do?

Ellen sits at the table

Ellen We get organized. It's too late to think of moving now so
  we'll stay here the night and assess the situation in the morning.

In the meanwhile, we have got to be practical. Sue, check what we have got in that room.

Sue Right.

Sue goes out to the bunkroom

Ellen There is a huge tank of water, I should think about ten thousand gallons, at the back of the building. Sheena you had better try and find a couple of buckets and bring them in here. Pearl, you . . . Oh well, you had better take it easy for a time. Now we ought to get a fire going. Marcia you had better . . .

Marcia moves angrily to the table

At this moment Sue returns from the bunkroom

Marcia (*angrily*) Who the hell are you giving orders to?

Ellen stands to face her

Ellen (*coldly*) I beg your pardon?

Marcia What gives you the right to assume leadership of the party?

Ellen (*coldly*) My husband happens to be Camp Superintendant, or had you forgotten?

Marcia So?

Ellen Which makes me the senior person.

Marcia (*forcefully*) We are not in camp now, we are a survival group, every person for herself, and I don't give a goddam sod whether your husband is the superintendant or the bloody office boy.

Ellen (*angrily*) How dare you speak to me like that . . .

Marcia moves a little towards her

Marcia (*forcefully*) Now get this, Ellen, and get it straight, no-one tells anyone to do anything. Everything from now on is done by common consent. That way we have a sporting chance of coming out of this. Everyone agreed?

Pearl Suits me.

Sue Me too.

Marcia Sheena?

Sheena (*hesitantly*) Well—I can see Ellen's point of view.

Marcia (*disgustedly*) Oh for God's sake . . .

*Marcia moves away with her back to them, annoyed. There is an
awkward pause*

Sue Er—there are six bunks and tons of blankets in there. It
must be where the vaqueros sleep when they bring the cattle
down.
Marcia (*shortly*) Well, if nothing else, we have got somewhere to
sleep tonight.
Sheena Do you think that is a good idea?
Sue Why not?
Sheena Well I've always understood that the safest place in an
earthquake was in the open. It's only just struck me that we
ran for shelter to the only building in sight.
Marcia That's quite a point. What do you suggest?
Sheena As we appear to have plenty of blankets, wouldn't we be
better off sleeping in the open?
Marcia You are probably right.

Ellen moves to the outer opening and peers out

Ellen I don't think that is very practical.
Sheena Why not?
Ellen I don't know if it is something to do with the earth tremors
but the place is alive with snakes. I saw three or four *fers de
lance* when I was outside just now.

There is a momentary silence

Pearl I can't stand snakes, so it's the bunkroom for me; and if it
comes down on top of me it's just too bad.
Marcia I'll join you.
Sue Me too.
Sheena I'm not very happy about it but it does seem the lesser
of two evils.
Marcia Which leaves you, Ellen.

Ellen shrugs resignedly

Ellen I suppose so.

There is a dull rumble which gets louder

Sue (*terrified*) Oh God, not again.

Suddenly all the women start to sway. Sheena screams. The pile of

*beer crates down left comes crashing down. All the women cry out
as they are thrown to the floor bringing the table and chairs with
them as the dust rises. It is all over in a few seconds; the silence
is broken by the quiet sobbing of Sheena. Cautiously, they get up
with the exception of Sheena who remains half sitting on the floor.
There is a pause*

(*anxiously*) Are you all right, Pearl?
Pearl Yes.

Marcia glances at the ceiling then round the room generally

Marcia If it will take that it will take anything. We are lucky this
    place is made of timber and not concrete.
Sue (*quietly*) We risk it, then?
Marcia I don't think we've any choice.

*Silently, they start to move into the bunkroom. Sheena remains half
sitting, her face buried in her hands. Marcia goes back to her*

Marcia (*kindly*) Come on, Sheena.

Sheena shakes her head

Sheena (*quietly, desperately*) I—I can't—I'm too frightened.
Marcia (*gently*) We all are.

*Marcia helps Sheena to her feet and she crosses slowly to the
door of the bunkroom. Marcia follows her but stops at the door
and turns to speak to Ellen who is rather isolated by the opening
left. Changing her mind she stares at Ellen for a moment then
goes out after Sheena. Ellen hesitates for a moment then slowly
moves to the door and into the bunkroom*

The Lights fade and the music comes up

Scene 2

The same. Dawn, the following morning

*As the Lights come up, Ellen is discovered picking up chairs, etc.
Sue enters from the bunkroom*

Sue I never heard you get up.

Ellen I couldn't sleep. Give me a hand, will you?

Together they pick up the table, chairs and boxes

That looks better.

Sue (*apprehensively*) For how long? (*She collects a beer crate from down left and carries it across to one side, where she puts it on the floor. From now on this becomes her "territory" in the room*)

Ellen I've got a feeling we are over the worst, there hasn't even been a small tremor since last night.

Sue Tell me something.

Ellen Yes.

Sue Were you scared last night? I mean, you seemed so calm.

Ellen (*quietly*) I've never been so frightened in my life.

Sue Me too. It's terrifying, isn't it, you become completely disorientated, you haven't even got control over your limbs; and do you know what scares me most? The eerie silence that follows, almost as if nothing had happened.

Ellen (*quietly*) Yes. (*She pauses. Almost as if she is changing the subject*) This place is filthy isn't it?

Sue Frankly I hadn't noticed. One thing is certain, I'm not doing any housework.

Ellen turns to her, laughing

Ellen What a ridiculous thought.

Sue Do you realize that's the first time anyone has laughed since the accident?

Marcia enters from the bunkroom

Marcia Oh you've finished, I was just coming to give you a hand.

Ellen It didn't take a minute.

Sheena enters from the bunkroom

Sheena Why didn't anyone wake me up?

Sue There wasn't any point, and we thought the rest would do you good.

Sheena I suppose it's reaction, but I haven't slept so soundly for years.

Marcia We'll leave Pearl there for the time being.

Sheena She isn't there..

Marcia What!
Sheena I thought she was out here with you.
Marcia (*quietly concerned*) Oh my God!
Sue What's the matter?
Marcia In her state of mind she's probably wandered off; she could be anywhere.
Ellen (*quickly*) You are right. Come on, we've got to find her.

They all start to make a move to the outer doorway, but fall back

Pearl enters. She carries two buckets and is over-cheerful. She moves behind the table

Pearl Oh, so you have all decided to get up, have you?
Ellen Where have you been?
Pearl On the scrounge. I don't know about you, but I am bloody hungry.
Sue Me too, now that you mention it.
Ellen How is your head?
Pearl Pretty rough but I can remember everything now. Here take that. (*She hands Sue a bucket of water*)
Sue What's this?
Pearl What the hell do you think it is? Water.

Sue takes the bucket and puts it on the floor upstage, then returns to the table and sits

You must excuse the child, she's simple. (*To Sue*) You've got the choice of tea, coffee, cocoa, or hot chocolate. The trouble is, they are all off, so you've got the only thing left on the menu.
Sue Ah, I get it. And what about my toast and marmalade? No, don't tell me, they have forgotten to deliver the bread?
Pearl Bright girl, so we have the next best thing.

Marcia half sits on the end of the table. Pearl dips into the other bucket and takes out some earthenware mugs which are not too clean and some large, square, hard-tack biscuits

There you are, girls. I've washed the mugs, sort of that is, so all you have to do is to dip into the bucket. There is no cover charge. Oh, and we've got tons of these if you are interested.
Sheena Where did you find all this?
Pearl There is a sort of cookhouse at the back with an old iron

range and piles of logs. We shan't starve either, there is enough
tinned food to keep us going for ages.
Ellen (*firmly*) But we are not stopping.

They all turn and stare at her

I mean, what's the point? We've got to try and get back—well,
haven't we?
Marcia (*quietly*) There's no hurry.
Ellen Maybe not, but what is the point in staying?

Marcia stands

Marcia Because it is the soundest thing to do.
Sheena Why?
Marcia On the same principle of an air crash. You stay by the
plane. When it is long overdue they send out a search party.
Ellen If there is anyone left to send.
Sheena That's a point, I hadn't thought of that.
Marcia (*persisting*) We have got to assume that until we know
they are not coming.
Ellen And how are we to know that?
Marcia (*angrily*) How the hell do I know? All I am saying is that
we have got to give them a chance and not complicate things
by moving away.
Sue I think you are right.
Ellen I still don't see . . .
Marcia (*coldly*) Ellen, I'm not going to argue. They have got two
helicopters at the camp. If they are not damaged, they will
start looking for us.
Sheena They knew at the camp that we went to Marimba.
Marcia Exactly, so that will be their first objective.
Sue Go on.

*Marcia kneels and marks out the route in the dust on the floor as she
explains*

Marcia When they find we are not there they will follow the road
back. When they come to where the landslide blocks the road
they will follow the track we took, and then they will see the
abandoned vehicle.
Sheena You make it sound so simple.
Marcia Not simple. Logical.

Ellen There is one thing you have overlooked. Supposing Marimba went with the quake? More important still, supposing the camp doesn't exist any more?

Marcia gets up, walks angrily to the outer door and stares out

Marcia I had thought of that. All I'm saying is that if anyone is still there, we must give them a chance of locating us.

Ellen, angry at being brushed off, goes up to Marcia, determined to carry on the fight

Ellen Now you listen to me, Marcia . . .

Pearl, anticipating trouble, breaks in

Pearl (*quietly*) We are a pretty selfish lot, aren't we?
Sue What made you say that?
Pearl We have been so concerned over our own safety that we haven't even given a thought to our men and the camp staff. For all we know they may be dead.
Sheena Don't, please . . . (*Upset, she moves to the box Sue placed and sits dejectedly*)
Pearl It's a thought, if nothing else.
Sue I won't go along with that. All the fellows were sleeping out in tents in open country. At the worst they are probably marooned like us.
Pearl Yes—yes I think you are right. They are probably not even as well off as us. At least we've got some grub; let's enjoy it. (*She bites at a biscuit then takes it out untouched*) Strooth!
Sheena What?
Pearl They are like iron.

Sue bites on a biscuit

Sue My God, you are right. I can't even dent it.
Pearl We'll just have to boil them or something. In the meantime I'll see if I can rustle up something else. (*She is about to move, when Marcia speaks*)
Marcia (*quietly*) Later.
Pearl There is no point in waiting.
Marcia I said later.

Sue looks at Marcia, who is still staring out of the opening. She gets up and moves a little to Marcia

Sue What are you looking at, Marcia?
Marcia The vultures are beginning to circle the vehicle.
Sue (*quietly*) Manuel, for a moment I had forgotten. (*She moves to Marcia to look out*)
Sheena (*standing*) What are you talking about?
Marcia (*quietly*) Before we do anything else we have got to bury him.

There is a long pause. Ellen moves to the table and sits

Sue The vehicle is a write-off, isn't it?
Marcia I should think so. What made you say that?
Sue As it's of no use to us, couldn't we—well . . .
Marcia Yes?
Sue Couldn't we set light to it and sort of—sort of cremate him?
Ellen (*matter-of-factly*) You can't do that.
Sue Why not?
Ellen Because it's company property. It may not be a write-off; perhaps the mechanics can put it back on the road again.

Marcia moves to Ellen angrily. She almost shouts

Marcia (*viciously*) There is a man out there, dead. He died trying to save us, and all *you* can think about is company property.
Ellen (*vehemently*) I didn't mean it like that.
Marcia Well what the hell did you mean, then?
Ellen (*wildly*) I mean—well there is nothing we can do for him, why not just leave him there?
Marcia And let the vultures have him?
Ellen No, but . . .
Marcia (*bitterly*) You'd bury a dog, wouldn't you?
Ellen Of course.
Marcia Well, what's more important, a man or a dog?

There is a silence. Ellen turns away

Ellen (*quietly*) I'm sorry, it's just that I can't stand the sight of blood, it makes me ill.

Marcia stares at her, disgusted. A pause

Pearl How are we going to dig a grave? We haven't anything to work with.

Sue moves to Pearl a little

Sue We—we could cover his body with rocks.
Marcia I think that is the most practical way.

Sheena moves to the table

Sheena (*quietly*) How are we going to get him out?
Pearl (*quietly*) He saved my life, I'll get him out—somehow.
Ellen (*softly*) I'll gather the rocks.
Sheena (*quietly*) I'll help you, Ellen.
Marcia When we have finished we'll collect our things from the
    vehicle and bring them back here; you never know what we
    might need. Everyone agreed?
Sue
Pearl } Yes. (*Speaking together*)

Marcia looks at them for a moment

Marcia (*quietly*) Let's get it over.

   Marcia goes out, followed by Pearl and Sue

*Sheena follows more slowly. She pauses at the door and turns to
Ellen, who is still sitting despondently at the table*

Sheena (*softly*) Ellen?
Ellen (*quietly*) I'm coming.

   *Sheena goes out. Ellen buries her face in her hands and gives a
   momentary shudder: she gets up, goes to the opening slowly, and
   follows the others*

The Lights fade, the music comes up

SCENE 3

The same. Two hours later

*Sue, Marcia, Pearl and Sheena enter from outside. They are all
tired, dusty and obviously under an emotional strain. They carry
their personal belongings, such as they are, and settle in silence, Sue
on the box she placed previously, the others about the room. After a
moment Sheena takes out a handkerchief and dabs the back of her
hand, which is bleeding slightly*

Pearl You've cut yourself.
Sheena I caught it on a sharp piece of rock.
Pearl Let's have a look.

Pearl takes hold of Sheena's hand: Sheena shrinks back

I'm not going to hurt you.
Sheena It's not that, it's—it's your hands . . .

Pearl glances at her hands, which are covered in blood from Manuel

Pearl (*quietly*) I'm sorry, I didn't realize. I'd better wash.

Pearl goes out through the outer opening

Marcia Is it bad, Sheena?
Sheena No, it looks worse than it is.
Marcia (*rising*) We'd better clean it up all the same, you can't be too careful, there could be a real risk of tetanus in a place like this.
Sheena Look, I'm scared enough as it is without your bright remarks.
Marcia (*smiling*) Sorry, only I feel we should bear it in mind. Give me your hankie. (*She takes it, dips it in the bucket of water then cleans up the scratch*) There, that looks a little better. What we really need now is some form of disinfectant.
Sue I've just remembered, I brought the first-aid kit from the car.
Marcia Great. Let's have it.

Sue passes it to her. Marcia opens it

Well that's helpful, just a couple of bandages. Have you got any toilet-water or anything?
Sheena I've a small bottle of eau de cologne.
Marcia That will do. Let's have it.

Sheena gives it to her

Sheena What do you want it for, anyway?
Marcia It's mostly spirit, which is the next best thing. Hold still, this may sting.

She shakes a generous amount over the wound. Sheena winces visibly

Sheena Ooh! You are not joking are you?

Marcia There you are, now we'll put one of these on—hold on, I've found something better, a plaster. (*She peels off the back and puts the plaster on Sheena's hand*) There. Incidentally, when did you have your last tetanus jab?
Sheena About five years ago.
Marcia (*cheerfully*) Oh well, if you don't die within the next few days, you should make it.
Sheena That of course has made my day.

Marcia returns the first-aid box to Sue then glances round

Marcia Where is Ellen?
Sue She stayed behind to make a rough cross from some branches.
Marcia (*quietly*) That's a nice thought.
Sheena You sounded as if you really meant that.
Marcia I did.
Sheena I thought you hated her.
Marcia Not her, the system. In the camp she is the boss lady because her husband holds the senior rank. She is so used to being the queen that she probably doesn't realize how overbearing she is, and we all go along with it for peace and quiet. But suddenly when we are plunged into a situation like this we are all naked and vulnerable and rank doesn't mean a damn thing.
Sue I know exactly what you mean.

Ellen enters from outside. She moves to her box to drop her carrier, then notices Sheena's hand

Ellen You have hurt yourself, Sheena.
Sheena It's only a scratch. Marcia fixed it up for me.

Ellen nods then turns away to search for something in her carrier. There is a pause while Marcia stares at her. Suddenly she speaks

Marcia (*suddenly*) I'm sorry for letting fly this morning, Ellen. I apologize.
Ellen (*looking up*) That's all right, it was my own fault. I don't know what made me make that stupid remark about saving the vehicle. (*She sits on the box, speaking without looking at them*) As if it mattered. I suppose the truth is that I didn't want to face up to Manuel's death. It's something I have always found repugnant, especially if it is violent.

Marcia I can understand that. (*She half sits on the front of the table*) The odd thing about death is that no-one ever wants to talk about it. A man's wife dies and he gets a week off from the office to get everything settled at home, but when he comes back no-one ever mentions his loss, and he never talks about it. It's all so unreal, almost as if it never happened. (*She opens a small wallet and stares at it for a moment*)

Sue What's that?

Marcia Manuel's wallet. (*She takes out a photograph*) I think this must be his wife and kids. (*Quietly*) We'll give it to her when we get back.

Sheena *If* we get back.

Ellen (*quietly*) We'll get back, Sheena—somehow.

Pearl bustles in from outside. She has washed her hands and arms. She is quite cheerful and carries some tins. She moves behind the table

Marcia moves away

Pearl I've just been having a shufti round the back and this place is pretty well stocked.

Sheena Was there any sign of anyone?

Pearl No, it was quite eerie, the place was quite obviously occupied just before the quake.

Sheena How do you know?

Pearl There are two half-eaten meals still on the table, just like the *Marie Celeste*. I reckon they got out mighty fast and the cattle stampeded, which will acount for the stockades being smashed; and there were definitely cattle there.

Sue How can you be so sure?

Pearl Well, I won't go into details but the evidence is still fresh.

Sheena Oh, charming!

They all suddenly laugh at Sheena's tone

Pearl You know this is quite a place really. They seem to have everything.

Sheena In your travels did you happen to notice a better loo?

Pearl No, there is another one but it is just as primitive as our present one. Two footprints in concrete and a bottomless pit.

Sheena I was afraid of that.

Sue Well, you have got the whole countryside at your disposal.
Sheena With the place crawling with snakes! Thanks, I'll take the black hole of Calcutta.
Pearl In the meanwhile, grub. There are cases of bully beef.
Sue Oh no.
Marcia Don't grumble, we are lucky to have them. What's in that one there?
Pearl I don't know. There's another case of these but they have no labels on them.
Ellen What do you suppose it is?
Pearl I don't know. I'm hoping it's fruit. (*She shakes it and listens*) It sounds like fruit.

Sue comes up to the table

Sue Open the damn thing, the suspense is killing me.
Sheena How *are* we going to open it?
Pearl With this. (*She produces a can-opener*) I told you, they have everything.

They gaze eagerly while Pearl opens a tin

Sue (*with a groan*) Oh no, it's beans.
Pearl Great. I love them, the trouble is they make me fart.
Ellen (*sharply*) Oh, don't be so crude.
Pearl Crude?
Ellen There is no necessity to resort to expressions like that.
Marcia What's wrong with it, it's a very expressive word.
Ellen (*standing angrily*) Trust you to stand up for her. Just because we happen to be in peculiar circumstances, there is no need to throw away all standards.
Marcia (*angrily*) What the hell have standards got to do with it? There is nothing wrong with a little harmless vulgarity, it relieves the tension.
Ellen If you can't see——
Sue (*interrupting quickly*) All right, all right, we've all got the point. Now let's drop it.

There is an awkward silence, broken by Sheena

Sheena I think it might be a good idea if we pooled everything we've got; there may be something useful without our realizing it.

Sue A good idea.

Sue goes to her box. Ellen goes back to her box. Sheena remains at the table as she has all her stuff at her feet. Marcia moves to her chair. Sue empties her handbag on the floor. It is full of lipsticks and useless objects

Marcia Good lord, how many lipsticks do you carry around with you?

Sue I don't know, I'm always buying new ones and never seem to throw the old ones away. Oh good, I've been looking for that key for weeks.

Pearl (*half sitting on the table*) The only thing I bought in Marimba was a frying-pan and we have got loads of those in the cookhouse.

Sheena I don't think I shall be much help either. I got these. (*She produces a pair of delicate shoes with thin high-heels*)

Sue Those should be ideal for climbing a mountain if we have to. Anything else?

Sheena Only this. (*She produces a large bottle of perfume*)

Sue Let's have a look. (*She goes to the table, takes the bottle and removes the top smelling the fragrance*) Cor, that's dead sexy.

Sue sprinkles a liberal helping of scent on her hands and arms then passes it to Marcia, who does the same

Pearl And me. (*She takes the scent from Marcia and does the same*)

Sheena Do you mind! That cost me a small fortune.

Sue Don't be mean, dear, we've got to be prepared in case the vaqueros come back.

Marcia (*smiling*) You should be so lucky.

Sue and Marcia return to their places again

Sheena What about you, Ellen?

Ellen The only thing I bought was a new phrase book.

Sheena Marcia?

Marcia Just a piece of material to make a dress. (*She sits on her chair and produces it from her carrier*)

Sue I'm not much better either, the only thing I got were these undies. (*She holds them up against herself*)

Marcia I've had a brilliant idea. Slip into them and stand outside the door, and we'll have a jumbo jet here in seven minutes flat.

Pearl gropes in her bag

Pearl Ah! I am about to produce the find of a lifetime.
Sue Don't tell me, a self-inflating hot-air balloon?
Pearl I've carried this around in my bag for years. Don't ask me why, it's a sort of talisman I suppose. There, how about that? (*She pulls out a small compass*)

Ellen rises and goes to Pearl

Ellen A compass! Now that really is something, Pearl; that may be very important to us.
Pearl You see, I'm not just a pretty face. Well, I don't know about you people but I'm starving. It won't take long to get a fire going and there is plenty of coffee.
Ellen No tea?
Pearl I didn't see any.
Ellen A pity. (*She sits*)
Pearl I'll get cracking and make a sort of hash for a start. I haven't been through all the stuff in the store yet but——
Marcia (*suddenly*) Quiet!
Pearl There are lots of packets of——
Marcia (*sharply*) Shut up, Pearl!
Pearl What the——

Marcia suddenly stands

Marcia (*urgently*) Listen!

They all listen. In the distance a plane is heard approaching

Sue (*quietly*) It's a plane—a plane . . . (*Shouting*) They have found us.

Suddenly the place erupts, they shout, laugh and yell. They all rush outside and yell at the top of their voices but after a few moments the sound of the plane dies away and they drift back into the room bitterly disappointed. Marcia goes to the table and bangs the top viciously in anger

Marcia (*angrily*) The blind stupid bastards, they must have seen us.
Sue I doubt it, they were on the far ridge.

Ellen They may not even have been looking for us.

Marcia Then we have to *make* them find us. Pearl, when you were looking around did you see any sacks of anything?

Pearl Not that I can remember.

Ellen There are some bags of lime in the yards.

Marcia Lime! That's it, something white. We'll mark out a huge S.O.S. on the ground; they can't miss that.

Ellen You are right.

Marcia Come on everyone, let's get moving. You never know, they may come back.

Inspired with new hope, they move out quickly talking among themselves

The Lights fade, the music comes up

SCENE 4

The same. Evening of the same day

Sheena enters from outside and sinks wearily into her chair at the table. She buries her head in her hands for a moment and then looks up to the ceiling in an almost silent prayer

Sheena (*almost in tears*) Oh God, help us, please I beg of you—help us.

Ellen appears in the outer doorway

Sheena is aware that someone is there and takes her bottle of perfume and puts some on her hands and arms. Ellen gives no indication of what she has just seen and moves above the table

Want some?

Ellen Thanks. Anything to take the smell of that lime away, it seems to penetrate everything.

Sheena I know. I've just had a shower but I can still smell it.

Ellen sits, resting her arms on the table

Ellen We made a good job of it though, the letters must be about twenty feet high and a foot thick. If they pass anywhere near they can't miss it.

A short pause

Sheena Ellen, do you really think they are looking for us?

Ellen Frankly, no.

Sheena What makes you say that?

Ellen Because there would have been a plane over by now if they were searching.

Sheena What do you think has happened?

Ellen I don't know, but I do think we are expecting too much too soon. As the men were in open country it is a fair bet that they came through it safely, but they still have a long journey back to camp before they can even start to organize a search party.

Sheena (*smiling*) You are a great comfort, I'm beginning to feel better already.

Ellen On the other hand, one must be brutally realistic about this. We don't know what damage there has been in the camp or if it even still exists for that matter. Even if it stands the helicopters may be damaged and out of action.

Sheena Even if they are, they can still travel by car.

Ellen I agree but how far? The road has completely disappeared in one huge land-slide. When they come to that what are they going to do? We are on the other side, but they don't know that.

Sheena So all we can really do is wait.

Ellen Yes, for the time being anyway. (*She gets up and moves away a little, glancing round the room*) Marcia is right when she says we ought to stay put and we are very lucky to have found a place like this. Can you imagine what it would have been like if it hadn't existed?

Sheena I'd rather not. (*Pause*) I'm sorry you and Marcia don't hit it off, it doesn't make things any easier.

Ellen No, especially when she is right.

Sheena I don't follow you.

Ellen Because of my husband's position with the company I have been—well—top dog, as you might say, among the women. Without realizing it one tends to manipulate the wives of the junior employees, and, there isn't much they can do about it, especially if they have their husband's future in mind. Because of this, you are all overbearingly nice to me.

Sheena We all do it, don't we?

Ellen Unconsciously, yes and there is a tendency for the top dog to become top bitch. (*She goes to the outer door and gazes through it*) It's only natural I suppose, chiefly because we live unnatural lives. Good food, air conditioning, decent housing and fat salaries never really compensate for uncomfortable heat, fever, lack of normal entertainment and living a two year stretch in a godless desert.

Sheena (*curiously*) Why are you telling me all this?

Ellen moves a little to Sheena

Ellen Because I've always taken everything for granted; but now, when it comes to the crunch, I realize how inadequate I am.

Sheena We all are.

Ellen No. For a start I don't have the organizing ability of Marcia, or the guts of Pearl for instance. It made me really ill to see her lug Manuel's body out of the truck by brute force, and he was horribly injured. I could never have done that, never—but she did. I felt utterly useless, and you all knew it because I walked away to be sick.

Sheena We understood. I couldn't have done it myself.

Ellen moves towards her box

Ellen Maybe, but it doesn't alter the fact that the so-called "Boss Woman" is a complete loss at a time when she is most needed.

Sue enters from outside. She is wearing a bra and slip, with her dress slung over her shoulder. She dries her hair with a filthy towel. She moves above the table

Sue Phew, this lime stinks, doesn't it?

Sheena We were just saying that. Here, try some of this. (*She hands her some perfume*)

Sue Ta. Sure you don't mind?

Sheena I do, but in the circumstances I'll forget it. What a filthy towel.

Sue It's better than nothing. God knows what I will catch, but I have got to dry my hair with something. I was going to have a swim in the tank, but Pearl made some rather rude remarks which put me off.

Sheena I can imagine. After all, we have to drink the stuff.

Sue Now don't you start.

Ellen Where's Marcia?

Sheena She had a shower then went back to the hill, she's been there all day. Pearl took her some food but she didn't eat it—

which reminds me, I'm starving. (*She goes to the outer opening and yells*) Come on, Pearl. (*To Sue*) What is she doing?

Sue I suspect one of her specialities. It will either be a wet hash or a dry hash, but right now I could eat either.

Pearl enters from outside

Pearl Did you call?

Sue Yes. My tummy is rumbling. What have we got for supper?

Pearl What would you like?

Sue (*thinking it out*) I'll start with melon, with prawn cocktail to follow, then fillet steak with *sauté* potatoes.

Pearl We are out of potatoes.

Sue Oh hell, well in that case I'll have a mixed salad.

Pearl How about a sweet?

Sue Strawberries and cream with black coffee and brandy to follow.

Pearl Is that all?

Sue For the time being. After all that, what are we having?

Pearl (*shortly*) Beans on toast.

Sue moves to her box and sits

Sue Oh no.

Pearl Oh yes, except that there isn't any toast; we haven't any bread.

Marcia enters from outside

Marcia Bread, I never eat it normally but right now I miss it more than anything else. Stupid isn't it?

Sheena No, I feel the same. I've cut out bread altogether on this diet of mine, but right now I could eat a whole loaf.

Ellen Is there any alternative to beans, Pearl?

Pearl Bully beef, *but* I have found something else which looks promising.

Sheena What?

Pearl It's a bottle of something, and it may be hooch.

Sue I don't believe it.

Pearl I'll get it.

Pearl exits outside

Ellen Do you know, I believe she would discover an ice cream parlour in the middle of the desert.

Sue All the same, I don't know what we would do without her, she's disgustingly practical.

Marcia sits wearily behind the table

Marcia I hope it's liquor, I could do with a drink, I feel quite drained.

Ellen (*quietly*) Why did you stay on the hill all day?

Marcia I don't know, I suppose I was hoping a plane would come over. I collected a lot of dead wood. I was going to make a fire if I heard anything.

Ellen That's a good idea.

Marcia Not really; the plane would have passed before I got it going.

Sheena What's the point of doing it, then?

Marcia I felt I had to do something.

Ellen It won't be wasted; we could get petrol and oil from the car and take it up there to throw on it. It would start an instant blaze.

Marcia Yes, you are right, I had forgotten about that.

Sue There is something else we could do, take the wheels off the car. The tyres would give off a lot of black smoke.

Marcia And I always thought you were an empty-headed twit.

Sue It takes a rude bitch like you to bring out the brilliance in me.

Marcia gets up with new interest, and moves to Sue a little

Marcia Seriously though, it's a great idea. First thing tomorrow we'll strip the wheels, siphon the petrol off and get it all up there. (*To Ellen*) That is, if you have no objection to our burning a little company property.

Ellen (*quietly*) That was unnecessary.

Marcia (*quickly contrite*) Yes, you are right. I'm sorry, it's just that . . . Oh, it doesn't matter.

Pearl enters with a very dirty-looking bottle

Pearl Here it is; for all I know it may well be disinfectant, but it's worth a try.

Pearl moves above the table. Marcia goes to her

Marcia Let's have it.

Marcia takes the bottle, and they all move round the table. Marcia removes the cork then sniffs

Sue Well?
Marcia I'm not sure. (*She puts a finger in the neck of the bottle and cautiously tastes the liquid on it. She smiles*)
Sheena What is it?
Marcia What I thought it was. Tequila.
Sue Honest?
Marcia Yes, it's as rough as guts, real fire water—but if it doesn't kill us it will make us feel a lot better.
Pearl (*presenting a mug*) Fine, mine's a pint.
Marcia Don't get too ambitious. Right, let's have your mugs.

They each take a mug from the table and Marcia pours a generous tot into each

Ellen, what about you?
Ellen (*quietly*) No, thanks.
Marcia Is this personal?
Ellen (*smiling*) No, I just don't like the stuff.
Marcia (*sincerely*) Have a drink—with me.

Ellen hesitates, then smiles

Ellen Yes. (*Quietly*) I'd like that.

Marcia pours her a tot. Ellen raises her mug

To the success of your beacon.
Marcia Thanks.
Sheena And to your tyres, Sue, may they make a lot of smoke.
Sue They will. (*Raising her mug*) And to the arrival of a new cook.
All (*laughing*) Here, here, etc.
Pearl Ungrateful bitches, I hope it gives you all the runs.
Sheena You'll be in the same boat.
Pearl Not me, mate, I've got cast-iron guts.

They all drink, and choke as it catches their throats

Sue Hell's teeth, fire water is right.
Sheena How do you suppose they make this stuff? (*Quickly*) No don't tell me, I'd rather not know.
Ellen When you have got over the initial shock it sets up a warm glow.

Sue You reckon? My bloody throat is on fire.
Pearl Don't expect any sympathy from me.

Marcia refills their mugs. Sue moves to her box and stands on it

Sue If only those vaqueros would return, we could have a wild
    party. You know, I've always read about group sex, it might be
    fun.
Sheena There's probably only a couple of them at best.
Sue So?
Sheena Two men and five women?
Sue When you have been stuck in a place like this for months it
    shouldn't be too much of a problem. (*She pulls the edge of her
    skirt up sexily with a broad grin*)
Ellen (*quietly, turning away*) Let's drop the subject, shall we?

*Sue makes a wry face at the others and gets down. Ellen sits on her
box*

I think we ought to look ahead.
Sheena Any ideas?
Ellen Well, despite our preparations with the beacon and S.O.S.,
    I feel we ought to make some plans, because although we have
    everything we want here I feel we can't stop indefinitely.
Marcia How long do you think we ought to give it?
Ellen I don't know; a few days, I suppose.
Sheena They are bound to find us by then.
Marcia There is no certainty about it at all.
Sue (*sitting on her box*) So, what do we do?
Marcia We have no alternative, we'll have to start walking.
Sheena But where?
Marcia We can't go back, the road is completely blocked, so
    there is only one way—(*moving to the outer opening*)—up over
    that mountain.
Sue How do we know which direction to take? We could be
    walking in circles without knowing it.
Marcia We have the normal landmarks, and on top of that we
    have Pearl's compass.
Ellen Of course, I had forgotten that.
Marcia We know the camp is roughly fifty miles in that direction,
    and if we could make about ten miles a day we could be there
    in about a week.

There is a pause

Sue What about food?
Pearl We've plenty of that, each one can carry her own rations.
Sue Water?
Pearl There's about a dozen water-bottles on slings in the cook-house, they obviously use them on cattle drives.
Marcia With luck we can refill them as we find water.
Ellen We shall need blankets as well, it's going to be mighty cold up there at night.

Marcia moves below the table and half sits

Marcia That's it, then. Providing we take our time and don't panic we should make it O.K. (*Pause*) I know one thing, if we do make it you will never see me back in the country again when my spell is over. I hate it.
Sheena Why did you come in the first place?
Marcia Because of Harry.
Ellen We come back to the old loyalty thing again.
Marcia Not in my case. (*She pauses and swigs the last of her drink*) Harry and I have been washed up for a long time. Harry's idea of a perfect wife is a deaf and dumb nymphomaniac with an off-licence. I didn't measure up to it. (*She pours herself another tot*)

No-one speaks

We decided to call it a day, but I needed capital. At my time of life I have lost the zest to make the big time the hard way. We made an agreement that I should come out here for his two year spell, and out of his salary of seventeen thousand a year he would give me five thousand. By the time his tour was over we would get a divorce and I would have ten thousand to set me up. (*She drinks*)
Sheena And I always thought you were such a devoted couple.
Marcia One has to be civilized, there is no point in fighting day and night for two years. Strangely enough, we find each other quite good company, but despite appearances we live a brother and sister existence.
Sue (*quietly*) Well I'm damned.
Marcia That surprises you?

Sue Yes. Like Sheena, I never suspected.
Marcia Why should you? That, in a nutshell, is my main reason
  for coming out of this alive. I've done fourteen months of my
  sentence and I am determined not to be cheated out of the rest ...
  Oh hell!

*Marcia suddenly throws her mug away quite viciously and walks
out to the bunkroom*

Sheena (*rising*) Marcia!
Ellen (*quietly*) Let her go.

Sheena sits again, slowly

Sheena Did you know?
Ellen No, but it explains a lot.

There is a pause

Pearl (*quietly*) The light is beginning to go, I'd better get supper
  cooked.
Sue (*quietly*) I'll come and give you a hand.

Pearl exits through the outer opening. Sue follows her

There is a pause

Sheena You never know, do you?
Ellen No.

The Lights fade, the music comes up

SCENE 5

The same. Dawn, four days later
*Sue is standing by the outer opening, smoking a cigarette. After a
moment Marcia enters from the bunkroom. Sue half turns*

Sue Hi.

*Marcia nods and searches in her bag, finds an empty packet of
cigarettes which she screws up and throws away*

Marcia Damn!
Sue Are you out?

Marcia Yes. I thought I had one left. How many have you got?
Sue This is my last one. Here, let's share it, we can take a drag in turn.
Marcia Are you sure?
Sue What the hell, I've been trying to kick the habit for years.

They meet at the table, Marcia takes the cigarette, inhales then hands it back

Marcia That's great. Thanks.

Sue wanders back to the entrance again, and Marcia half sits on the table

Sue?
Sue Yes.
Marcia Nothing ever seems to ruffle you. How do you do it?
Sue Probably because I've got no imagination.
Marcia The strain is beginning to tell now, and we are all pretty edgy; even small things get blown up out of proportion but you just seem to shrug them off. I envy you.
Sue (*handing her the cigarette again*) I'll tell you something which may surprise you. I was terrified when we first got here, but once we had settled down and there were no more tremors, I got to like the place—in fact I enjoy being here.
Marcia You enjoy it!
Sue Yes, it's a sort of challenge. We are always hoping that something good is just round the corner. I find it stimulating.
Marcia I never thought of it like that.
Sue If we were back in camp right now we would probably be bitching and at each other's throats as usual out of sheer boredom—but here you never know what is round the corner. A plane might come over—other people might turn up caught in the same way as we were—the vaqueros might return. There are so many possibilities.
Marcia Aren't you scared at all?

Sue sits at the table

Sue Oh, I have my moments of despair; I mean, like the other day when we built that beacon all ready to light. I firmly believed we would get a plane over the same day: but it's been four days now with—nothing.

Marcia (*quietly*) You are beginning to wonder if there is anyone or anything left out there?
Sue Yes. (*Cheerfully*) Perhaps they will come today.
Marcia (*quietly*) Perhaps. (*She leans over and touches Sue's hand lightly with a little smile*)

Sheena enters from the bunkroom

Sheena Morning.

They nod

You know one of the things I'm looking forward to when we get back? A bubble bath. I shall soak in it for hours. These blankets are very warm but I shudder to think when they were last cleaned, if ever.

Pearl enters from the bunkroom

Pearl (*crossly*) Why didn't someone wake me up?
Sheena What's the point?
Pearl (*shortly*) Well, you want breakfast, don't you?
Sheena (*shortly*) Does it matter what time we have it?
Pearl No, but ...
Sheena Oh don't be so damn pernickety about it.
Pearl (*angrily*) If that's your attitude, you can get your own bloody grub in future.
Sheena (*tersely*) You were the one to take it on in the first place, no-one pressured you into it.
Pearl That's not the point. The fact is——
Marcia O.K. Let's leave it alone.
Pearl (*angrily*) That's all very well ...
Marcia (*harshly*) I said leave it alone.

Pearl subsides. Marcia speaks quietly

We are all very grateful to you, Pearl. In the circumstances you have done marvels.

Pearl gives her a little nod of gratitude then goes off through the outer opening

Sheena (*irritably*) Why do you always take her side?
Marcia (*angrily*) I'm not taking anyone's side, but what's the point in fighting over trivial issues? Let's stick to practical

things. For a start, see if you can raise anything on your radio.
Sheena It's a waste of time.
Marcia Nothing is a waste of time, anything is worth trying.

*Sheena goes to get her radio. Sue takes it from the carrier on the
floor and hands it to her. She almost snatches it from her*

Sheena (*crossly*) And you leave my things alone.

*Sue shrugs her shoulders then goes to her box and sits. Sheena
switches on and moves the dials, there is no sound*

I told you. Nothing.

*There is a pause, then Sue picks up a magazine from beside her
box. It is very tatty and dog eared*

Sue (*cheerfully*) Oh, I forgot to tell you, I found this under my
mattress last night. It's a sort of Spanish *Playboy*. (*She flips
through the pages*) I tell you what, it puts the English version to
shame. (*Staring at a page*) Cor, what I wouldn't give to have
boobs like that. (*She stands to show it better to Marcia*) And
look at this one, these defy the laws of gravity.

*Sheena suddenly stands angrily. She goes to Sue and, snatching the
magazine from her, throws it away*

Sheena (*angrily*) Oh for God's sake, must you always harp on
sex? Anyone would think there was nothing else in life the way
you go on.
Sue (*smouldering quietly*) Pick that up.
Sheena (*shortly*) Pick it up yourself.
Sue (*her voice rising*) I said pick it up.
Sheena (*adamantly*) No.
Sue (*angrily*) You prissy bitch.
Sheena (*angrily*) Better that than a raving sex maniac.
Sue Geez!

*Sue suddenly flings herself on Sheena who collapses. They struggle
violently, fighting mad, on the floor, and shouting. Marcia shouts
at them and steps in to separate them. They sprawl there panting
with Marcia half-kneeling between them*

Marcia For God's sake, you two, cool it.
Sheena Well, she had no right . . .

Marcia Forget it, it's over.

Sheena That's all very well but . . .

Marcia I said forget it. It's nobody's fault, it's this place and everything that goes with it. (*She stands*) Look, we've probably got a really tough time ahead of us, and we can't afford any animosity.

Sue (*quietly*) You are right. I'm sorry Sheena.

Sheena (*a little ungraciously*) Oh, that's O.K.

They get up and dust themselves down. Sue goes to her box and sits.

Marcia moves to the bunkroom door

Marcia We'd better wake up Ellen, I suppose.

Sheena sits at the table

Sheena She's not there, she got up in the middle of the night.

Marcia Didn't you ask her where she was going?

Sheena Why should I? I thought she was going to the loo. In any case, I was only half awake.

Marcia Was she dressed?

Sheena I don't know.

Marcia (*coming back to the table*) Think, Sheena, think.

Sheena (*slowly*) Yes—now you mention it, she was.

Sue Why the panic?

Marcia Well, don't you see, she could be anywhere, bitten by a snake—anything. We all agreed to stick together with no-one going off on their own. Come on, we'd better find her.

Sue, Sheena and Marcia move towards the outer opening

Ellen appears in the outer opening. She carries something wrapped in old newspaper

We were just going to search for you. Where the hell have you been?

Ellen In the kitchen.

Marcia Doing what?

Ellen moves above the table

Ellen Making a surprise. You remember saying the other day that the only thing you'd like more than anything else would be a loaf of bread?

Marcia Yes.

Ellen (*happily*) Well, I've baked one.

Sue You've what?

Ellen (*triumphantly*) I've baked a loaf of bread.

Sue But how?

Ellen Yesterday I found a bag of flour in the kitchen, so I got up at about four this morning, got the stove going and made it.

Sheena But you haven't any yeast.

Ellen No, I realized that so I did the next best thing, I used the last of my Eno's salts.

They all laugh

Sue Did it work?

Ellen I don't think so, it doesn't seem to have risen at all. (*She takes the loaf out and puts it on the table*)

Marcia Never mind, it looks wonderful.

Ellen I've brought a knife. (*She hands a knife to Marcia*)

Marcia Oh no, it's yours, you must have the honour.

Ellen (*smiling*) I've heard of people launching ships before but never loaves. (*She tries to cut the loaf but cannot even penetrate the crust. Despairingly*) I can't cut it, it's solid.

Marcia Let me have a try. (*She tries, but has no luck. Frowning, she picks up the loaf*) It's pretty heavy.

Ellen I thought so, too.

Marcia wets her finger and puts it on the loaf then tastes it. She smiles

What?

Marcia This isn't flour Ellen, it's gypsum. They use it for soil-testing.

Sheena What's gypsum?

Marcia It's another name for plaster of Paris.

Sue Oh no.

Marcia 'Fraid so.

Suddenly they all see the funny side and relax in peals of laughter. Ellen stares at them for a moment then moves to her box, sits, buries her face in her hands and sobs. They stop laughing and Marcia goes to her, half-kneeling beside her

Hey, what's all this? We weren't laughing at you, Ellen, it was a mistake anyone could make.

Ellen (*bitterly*) Oh what's the use? I am a complete failure. I wanted so much to do something practical for us and—I'm just no good at anything.

Marcia Of course you are, and we appreciate what you did very much.

Sheena (*going to Ellen*) It was a lovely idea.

Sue I agree.

Pearl enters quickly from outside and moves above the table. For the first time, she seems upset

Pearl Listen, everyone . . .

Sheena (*shortly*) Not now, Pearl, later.

Pearl (*grimly*) If we hang about, mate, there may not be a later.

They all turn and stare at her

Marcia What's happened?

Pearl Nothing—yet.

Marcia Oh for God's sake let's cut out the guessing game.

Pearl I will if you give me a chance to tell you.

Ellen (*standing quietly*) Pearl, something serious has happened, what is it?

Pearl I finished packing the rations this morning and thought I'd have a last check of the vehicle to see if there was anything we might be able to make use of.

Sheena Did you get anything?

Pearl No, I couldn't reach the car—it's under six feet of water.

Sue (*aghast*) But how?

Pearl We haven't noticed anything as we are out of sight up here, but the river has spread everywhere these last few days.

Sheena But when we left it was only two hundred yards across.

Pearl I know—it is now about four miles wide.

Sue Four miles!

Pearl Yes, as far as you can see, all around.

Sheena (*a little hysterically*) We've got to do something!

Ellen (*sharply*) Quiet, Sheena.

Sheena Yes, but . . .

Ellen *firmly*) It won't help us if you or anyone else loses their heads. Go on Pearl.

Pearl It must be blocked solid somewhere between here and the coast, and that is causing this tremendous build up.

Marcia Well, if it's steady there is no immediate danger here.

Pearl I disagree. At the moment the only thing separating us from that vast lake is the landslide that came down in front of the vehicle, and the water is six feet up that already and seeping through fast at the bottom.

Sheena At least it's holding all right.

Pearl (*harshly*) But for how long? There's thousands of tons weight behind that lot; it could go at any time.

Ellen (*quietly*) From what you saw, how long *do* you think it will hold?

Pearl It's impossible to say. Luckily there is no wind, so there's no movement on the water. It's like a solid glass sheet as far as you can see. There are no birds, no sign of life at all, not even a sound. It's terrifying.

Ellen How high do you reckon we are up here?

Pearl About a hundred feet or so.

Marcia What are you getting at, Ellen?

Ellen I'm trying to work out the risk element. I think we are high enough up here. Even if our own little dam does go it will probably do so gradually, as there is no water turbulence to smash it down. It will then start to fill up the valleys below us.

Marcia I see what you mean.

Sheena I don't.

Ellen What I am saying is that after the first surge of water as the dam goes, it will settle down to a new level before building up again, which gives us time to get organized. Talking of which, Pearl, are the rations all ready?

Pearl Yes, I've packed five identical bags with enough food to keep us going for about ten days.

Ellen Water?

Pearl Each one has two sling water-bottles. Everything is ready, all we have to do is to pick them up.

Ellen (*quietly*) Well, this is it then. I don't think there is much point in waiting any longer.

Sheena, now really frightened, starts to get a little hysterical; this builds as the argument ensues

Sheena (*her voice rising a little*) But we don't have to leave at this minute, do we?

Ellen I think it advisable.

Sheena (*a little wildly*) But you said you didn't think we were in any immediate danger.

Ellen Yes.

Sheena (*forcefully*) Well, another half day won't make any difference, will it?

Marcia Why take the risk?

Sheena I don't think there is any real risk. As Pearl said, we are at least a hundred feet above the water level and it would give us that little extra time to be found even now.

Pearl (*angrily*) Just how bloody stupid can you be? What do I have do to do to convince you? If you think you are so snug and safe here, just go down to the dam and take a look for yourself.

Sheena (*wildly*) It's only your opinion—you are trying to panic us. Can't you see we are safe here, but out there on that mountain who knows what we'll come up against—and—and—and the place is full of snakes. (*To Ellen, accusingly*) You told us the first day, remember?

Ellen It's a small risk.

Sheena (*hysterically*) Small! What right have you to . . .

Marcia (*harshly*) Shut up, do you hear, shut up!

Sheena (*shouting*) It's all very well for you to talk, you have nothing to lose if we don't make it, but I've got a husband and family and . . .

Pearl (*shouting*) Sheena, Sheena, if you are too blind to see . . .

Suddenly there is a loud muffled explosion in the distance followed by a sustained deep rumbling. They stand for a moment in shocked silence

Marcia The dam—it's gone!

They rush to the opening, gazing out

Sue (*horrified*) My God, just look at that wall of water, it must be thirty feet high!

Suddenly they all become a little hysterical not quite knowing what to do or where to go. Their voices rise. Ellen suddenly takes command

Ellen Quiet. Everyone quiet!

They stop and look at her

(*Firmly*) We are *not*, I repeat *not* in any immediate danger. Go and collect your blankets as quickly as possible then come back here.

All but Ellen go quickly into the bunkroom

Ellen stares for a moment at the water, then goes to her box and gathers up her carrier

The others enter, each carrying blankets

Sue I've brought yours, Ellen. (*She puts them on the table*)

Ellen Thank you. Now get your belongings and we'll meet up at the cookhouse. Pearl will give you your rations and water, and it might be a good thing to have a really long drink before we leave.

Pearl Right. (*To the others*) Come on.

Pearl goes out, followed by Sheena and Sue

Marcia puts a few things in her carrier and Ellen goes to the table and puts a sheet of paper on it

Marcia What's that?

Ellen It's a kind of record; I've headed it. "To whoever finds this", and the date. I've given our names, how we came to be here and why we are being forced to leave. It may never be found, but I think we ought to leave something.

Marcia (*quietly*) You have come into your own, you are a born leader.

Ellen (*quietly grateful*) With your help, I can be.

Marcia leans over, takes Ellen's pen from her and writes a line at the bottom of the page

What have you written?

Marcia I've merely added, "We have gone on".

Marcia returns Ellen's pen to her

Ellen picks up her blankets from the table, takes her carrier, and goes out. Marcia follows her, but pauses at the opening for a last glance at the room: she looks at her carrier, then, with a shrug, tosses it into the room and goes out, as—

the CURTAIN *falls*

FURNITURE AND PROPERTY LIST

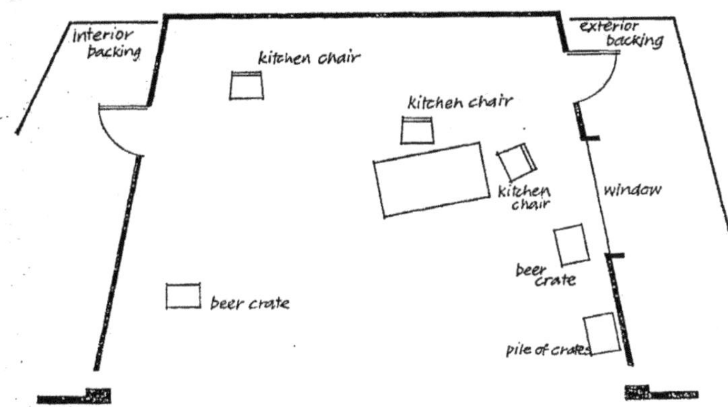

On stage: Old rough wooden table
3 kitchen chairs
Pile of beer crates
On floor: dust, dirt, general rubbish
On walls: cut-out pictures from "girlie" magazines

Off stage: Bucket of water **(Pearl)**
Bucket with 5 earthenware mugs and hard tack biscuits
(Pearl)
Blood sponge **(Pearl)**
First-aid kit, with 2 bandages and sticking-plaster **(Sue)**
Manuel's wallet **(Marcia)**
Unlabelled bean tins and tin opener **(Pearl)**
Dirty towel **(Sue)**
Dirty bottle of tequila **(Pearl)**
Loaf of "bread" (gypsum) wrapped in newspaper, and knife
(Ellen)
5 lots of blankets **(Pearl, Sue (2), Marcia, Sheena)**
Tatty "girlie" magazine (*To be set beside Sue's box for Scene
5*)

Personal: **Pearl:** handbag and carrier with personal possessions including compass

Sue: handbag and carrier with personal possessions including underclothes, lipsticks, key, cosmetic oddments. Cigarette (*for Scene 5*)

Ellen: handbag and carrier with personal possessions including phrase book, paper, pencil

Sheena: handbag and carrier with personal possessions including handkerchief, eau de cologne, high-heeled shoes, bottle of perfume, portable radio

Marcia: handbag and carrier with personal possessions including dress material, empty cigarette packet (*for Scene 5*)

LIGHTING PLOT

Property fittings required: nil
Interior. A bare room

To open: General effect of early evening light
Cue 1   At end of Scene 1   (Page 8)
Fade to Black-out, then up to dawn light for Scene 2,
gradually brightening

Cue 2   At end of Scene 2   (Page 14)
Fade to Black-out, then up to mid-morning light for
Scene 3

Cue 3   At the end of Scene 3   (Page 21)
Fade to Black-out, then up to early evening light for
Scene 4

Cue 4   **Marcia:** "Not in my case."   (Page 28)
Start fade to dusk

Cue 5   At end of Scene 4   (Page 29)
Fade to Black-out, then up to dawn light for Scene 5,
gradually brightening

EFFECTS PLOT

MADE AND PRINTED IN GREAT BRITAIN BY
LATIMER TREND & COMPANY LTD PLYMOUTH
MADE IN ENGLAND

www.ingramcontent.com/pod-product-compliance
Ingram Content Group UK Ltd.
Pitfield, Milton Keynes, MK11 3LW, UK
UKHW021817150726
7214IPUK00017B/177